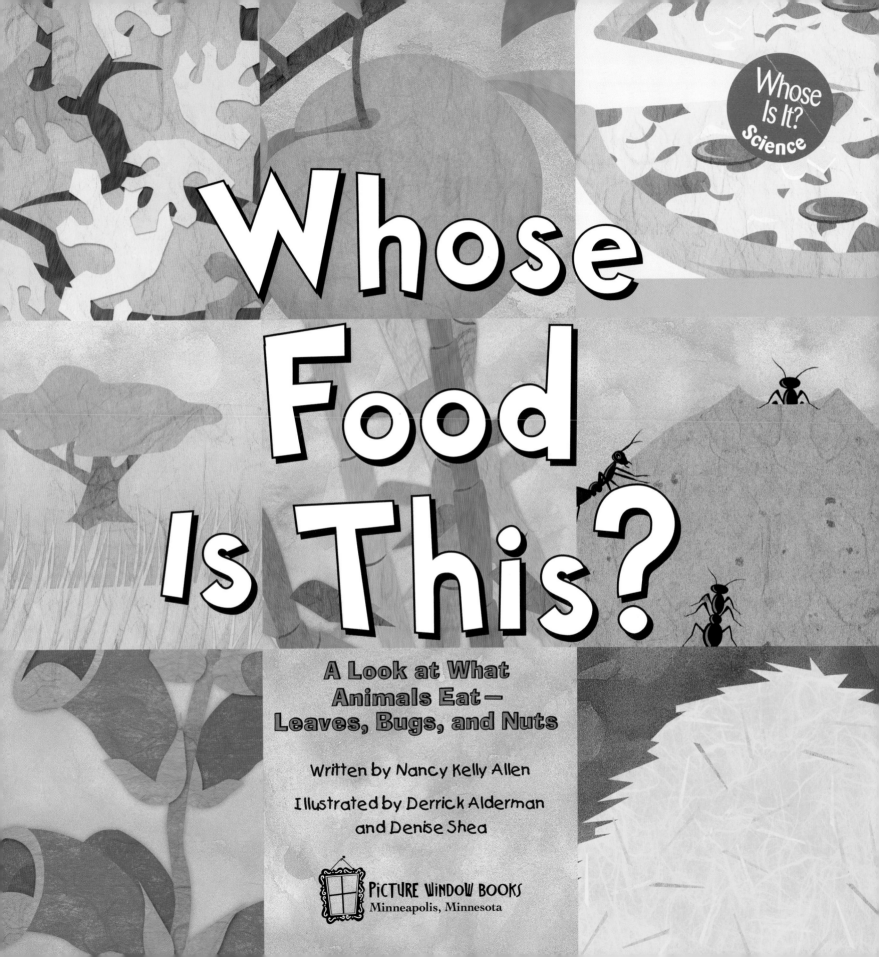

Whose Food Is This?

A Look at What Animals Eat— Leaves, Bugs, and Nuts

Written by Nancy Kelly Allen

Illustrated by Derrick Alderman and Denise Shea

PICTURE WINDOW BOOKS
Minneapolis, Minnesota

Whose Is It? Science

Special thanks to our advisers for their expertise:

Debbie Folkerts, Ph.D.
Assistant Professor of Biological Sciences
Auburn University, Alabama

Susan Kesselring, M.A., Literacy Educator
Rosemount-Apple Valley-Eagan (Minnesota) School District

Managing Editors: Bob Temple, Catherine Neitge
Creative Director: Terri Foley
Editors: Nadia Higgins, Patricia Stockland
Editorial Adviser: Andrea Cascardi
Storyboard Development: Amy Bailey Muehlenhardt
Designer: Nathan Gassman
Page production: Banta
The illustrations in this book were prepared digitally.

Picture Window Books
5115 Excelsior Boulevard
Suite 232
Minneapolis, MN 55416
877-845-8392
www.picturewindowbooks.com

Printed in the United States of America.

Library of Congress Cataloging-in-Publication Data
Allen, Nancy Kelly, 1949-
Whose food is this : a look at what animals eat—leaves,
bugs, and nuts / by Nancy Kelly Allen ; illustrated by Derrick
Alderman and Denise Shea.
p. cm. — (Whose is it?)
Includes bibliographical references and index.
ISBN 1-4048-0607-5 (reinforced lib. bdg. : alk. paper)
1. Animals—Food—Juvenile literature. I. Alderman, Derrick
II. Shea, Denise. III. Title. IV. Series.

QL756.5.A46 2004
591.5'3—dc22
2004000862

Let's get a taste of who's who.

Look closely at an animal's food. Animal food can be creeping bugs or juicy fruit. It can be a tender plant or a tough nut.

Some animals are picky eaters. Others eat all kinds of things. Some animals carefully chew their food. Others slurp it up or swallow it whole.

Animal foods don't all look alike because animals don't all eat alike.

Can you feed the food to the right animal?

Look in the back for more fun facts about food.

Whose food is this, fallen on a leafy lawn?

4

These are a squirrel's acorns.

A squirrel is nutty about nuts. In autumn, it buries acorns and other nuts in the ground. When winter comes, it digs them up. A squirrel can smell a buried nut under a thick blanket of snow.

Fun fact: A squirrel can tell if a nut is wormy just by smelling it. If a nut has a worm, the squirrel tosses it away.

Whose food is this, crawling up a tiny hill?

7

These are an anteater's ants.

An anteater digs in an anthill with its strong claws.
It unrolls its long, sticky tongue. *Slurp!* It licks up
lots and lots of ants. An anteater can eat up to
30,000 insects in one day.

Fun fact: An anteater can't see
very well. It uses its sense of smell
to find anthills.

Whose food is this,
deep inside a tube-shaped flower?

This is a hummingbird's nectar.

A hummingbird flies over a flower. It dips its long, pointed beak into the flower's center. Yum! The bird gulps up the sticky, sweet nectar.

Fun fact: A hummingbird can fly backward and even upside down. That's a handy skill for a bird that finds food in hard-to-reach places.

Whose food is this,
so green and lush?

This is a giant panda's bamboo.

The panda crushes tough bamboo plants with its strong teeth and jaws. *Chomp, chomp, chomp.* A panda spends between 10 and 12 hours a day eating.

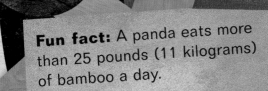

Fun fact: A panda eats more than 25 pounds (11 kilograms) of bamboo a day.

Whose food is this, piled up in a barn?

This is a cow's hay.

A cow has four stomachs. She swallows hay and grass without chewing very much. Later, the cow burps up the food and chews it more. She swallows it again, and it goes to another stomach. Lots of stomachs and extra chewing let a cow eat food that is too tough for other animals to eat.

Fun fact: A cow's burped-up food is called cud. When you see a cow that looks like it is chewing gum, it is probably chewing its cud.

Whose food is this, dangling from a tree?

15

This is a fruit bat's peach.

A fruit bat flies from tree to tree, eating peaches and other fruits. The bat chews the whole fruit. It swallows the soft, sweet parts. Then it spits out most of the pulp, seeds, and peel.

Fun fact: The fruit bat scatters seeds when it spits them out. This helps the fruit trees grow new plants.

Whose food is this,
scattered about an African field?

17

These are an ostrich's seeds.

An ostrich eats mostly seeds and grass. The wide, shallow beak of the ostrich is perfect for pulling up plants. It can yank up a big clump of grass in just one bite.

Fun fact: An ostrich doesn't have teeth, so it eats pebbles, too. The pebbles help crush the plants in a special part of the bird's stomach called the gizzard.

Whose food is this,
so gooey and good?

This is your piece of pizza!

You chomp on pizza and nibble on peas. You sip up soup. You gobble up watermelon and spit out the seeds. What else do you chew when your tummy starts rumbling?

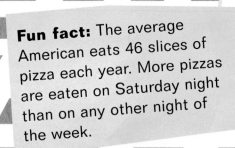

Fun fact: The average American eats 46 slices of pizza each year. More pizzas are eaten on Saturday night than on any other night of the week.

Just for Fun

The butter you buy at the store is made from a cow's milk.
Follow this recipe to make your own butter. (Get an adult to help you.)

What you need:

- a baby food jar with a tight lid
- a large spoonful of heavy whipping cream
- a slice of bread
- salt

What you do:

1. Put the whipping cream into the jar.

2. Cover the jar with the lid.

3. Now, shake it. Shake some more. Keep shaking!
   After 15 minutes or so, a lump of butter will form
   in the jar. (Two or more people can work together on one jar
   of butter, taking turns shaking it.)

4. Remove the lid.

5. Spread the butter on the bread. Add a little salt.

Happy Eating!

Fun Facts About Animal Food

More Honey, Please
The sloth bear is also called a honey bear. This bear can easily climb trees to steal honey from a beehive. The bear spends hours licking the sweet, sticky honey off its paws.

Any Plant Will Do
Fresh green grass and wildflowers are two of a tortoise's favorite foods. Another is fruit. A tortoise's diet varies according to where it lives. A desert tortoise loves to eat a prickly cactus.

Smells Delicious
A lizard smells with its tongue. The lizard sticks out its tongue to find food. Some lizards eat fruit and flowers, but most eat insects.

Forest Buffet
To a gorilla, the forest is like a big restaurant. Since a gorilla eats leaves, roots, seeds, and fruit, all it has to do is reach out and grab a meal. An adult gorilla can eat 50 pounds (22½ kilograms) of food a day.

A Helpful Eater
A ladybug eats tiny green insects called aphids, which are pests. Aphids eat healthy plants in gardens. This destroys the plants. Gardeners buy ladybugs by the bucket. By eating the aphids, these ladybugs help keep the plants green and growing.

Words to Know

bamboo—a plant with a strong, hollow stem

cud—the half-eaten food that a cow burps up and chews

gizzard—the part of a bird's stomach that is used for crushing food

nectar—the sweet liquid found inside flowers

pulp—the fleshy part of fruit

To Learn More

At the Library

Davis, Lee. *Feeding Time*. New York: Dorling Kindersley, 2001.

Fitzsimons, Cecilia. *Giant Pandas Eat All Day Long.* Brookfield, Conn.: Copper Beech Books, 2000.

Hickman, Pamela. *Animals Eating: How Animals Chomp, Chew, Slurp, and Swallow.* Toronto: Kids Can Press, 2001.

Knight, Tim. *Fantastic Feeders.* Chicago: Heinemann Library, 2003.

On the Web

FactHound offers a safe, fun way to find Web sites related to this book. All of the sites on FactHound have been researched by our staff. *www.facthound.com*

1. Visit the FactHound home page.
2. Enter a search word related to this book, or type in this special code: 1404806075.
3. Click the FETCH IT button.

Your trusty FactHound will fetch the best Web sites for you!

Index

Look for all the books in this series:

Whose Ears Are These?
A Look at Animal Ears—Short, Flat,
and Floppy

Whose Eyes Are These?
A Look at Animal Eyes—Big,
Round, and Narrow

Whose Feet Are These?
A Look at Hooves, Paws, and Claws

Whose Food Is This?
A Look at What Animals Eat—
Leaves, Bugs, and Nuts

Whose House Is This?
A Look at Animal Homes—Webs,
Nests, and Shells

Whose Legs Are These?
A Look at Animal Legs—Kicking,
Running, and Hopping

Whose Mouth Is This?
A Look at Bills, Suckers, and Tubes

Whose Nose Is This?
A Look at Beaks, Snouts, and Trunks

Whose Shadow Is This?
A Look at Animal Shapes—Round,
Long, and Pointy

Whose Skin Is This?
A Look at Animal Skin—Scaly, Furry,
and Prickly

Whose Sound Is This?
A Look at Animal Noises—Chirps,
Clicks, and Hoots

Whose Spots Are These?
A Look at Animal Markings—Round,
Bright, and Big

Whose Tail Is This?
A Look at Tails—Swishing,
Wiggling, and Rattling

Whose Work Is This?
A Look at the Things Animals
Make—Pearls, Milk, and Honey